Journey
to English

CARLA MAURÍCIO C. DA S. VIANNA
MARIANNA VEIGA TAVARES

3

WORKBOOK

MACMILLAN

© Carla Maurício C. da S. Vianna e Marianna Veiga Tavares, 2013

Diretora editorial: Ana Claudia Ferrari
Gerente editorial: Gisele Aga
Editora de arte: Simone Oliveira Vieira
Designer: Ivan Toledo Prado
Assistente de arte: Carol Duran
Pesquisadora iconográfica: Gabriela Farcetta
Coordenadora de produto: Carla Rodrigues Riquena
Assistente de redação: Elena Regina Pucinelli
Coordenadora de produção gráfica: Roseli Said

Editora de conteúdo: Luciana Macias Pimentel
Editores-assistentes: Fernando Santos, Silene Cardoso
Preparadora: Sâmia Rios
Revisor linguístico: Robert Caudler Garner
Projeto gráfico: Ivan Toledo Prado
Edição de arte e diagramação: Estúdio Sintonia
Capa: Ivan Toledo Prado
Ilustrações: Giz de Cera Studio (Sidney Meireles)
Iconografia: Etoile Shaw, Gabriela Farcetta, Odete Ernestina Pereira
Tratamento de imagens: Paulo César Salgado

Créditos das fotos:
Página 3: © Nilo Lima/Opção Brasil Imagens Página 5: © Michaeljun/Dreamstime.com; © Eastwest Imaging/Dreamstime.com; © Mrspants/Dreamstime.com; © Jaimie Duplass/iStockphoto/Thinkstock; © Dgilder/Dreamstime.com Página 11: © iStockphoto/Thinkstock; © iStockphoto/Thinkstock; © iStockphoto/Thinkstock; © iStockphoto/Thinkstock; © Connect1/Dreamstime.com; © 3dbrained/Dreamstime.com Página 13: © The World Almanac and Book of Facts, 2013. New York, Infobase Publishing; © Reprodução; © Daniel Augusto Jr/Pulsar Imagens; © Mrallen/Dreamstime.com; © Paramount Pictures/Album/Latinstock; © Kevin Winter/Getty Images Página 15: © iStockphoto/Thinkstock; © Comstock/Thinkstock; © iStockphoto/Thinkstock; © Hemera/Thinkstock; © iStockphoto/Thinkstock Página 17: © Franz Pfluegl/Dreamstime.com Página 20: © Popperfoto/Getty Images; © Coleção particular; © Gesellschaft der Musikfreunde, Viena; © David Borchart/The New Yorker Collection; © Barbara Smaller/The New Yorker Collection Página 21: © Frisket/Dreamstime.com; © Polka Dot/Thinkstock; © iStockphoto/Thinkstock; © Smikhailov/Dreamstime.com; © iStockphoto/Thinkstock; © Jupiterimages/Botanica/Getty Images Página 22: © Phil Dent/Redferns/Getty Images; © Ethan Miller/Getty Images Página 23: © Pete Souza/The White House Página 24: © Broken1984/Dreamstime.com; © Comstock Images/Thinkstock; © iStockphoto/Thinkstock; © Mphotographix/Dreamstime.com; © iStockphoto/Thinkstock Página 27: © Rido/Dreamstime.com

Todos os esforços foram feitos no sentido de encontrar os detentores dos direitos das obras protegidas por *copyright*. Caso tenha havido alguma omissão involuntária, a editora terá o maior prazer em corrigi-la na primeira oportunidade.

```
Dados  Internacionais  de  Catalogação  na  Publicação  (CIP)
        (Câmara  Brasileira  do  Livro,  SP,  Brasil)


        Vianna, Carla Maurício C. da S.
            Journey to English Workbook / Carla Maurício C.
        da S. Vianna, Marianna Veiga Tavares. -- 1. ed. --
        Cotia, SP : Macmillan, 2013.


            Obra em 4 v.
            ISBN 978-85-7418-880-5 (Journey to english 1 )
            ISBN 978-85-7418-937-6 (Journey to english 2 )
            ISBN 978-85-7418-938-3 (Journey to english 3 )
            ISBN 978-85-7418-939-0 (Journey to english 4 )


            1. Inglês (Ensino fundamental) I. Tavares,
        Marianna Veiga. II. Título.




13-04091                              CDD-372.652
```

           Índices para catálogo sistemático:

        1. Inglês : Ensino fundamental   372.652

MACMILLAN DO BRASIL
Rua José Félix de Oliveira, 383 – Granja Viana
Cotia – SP – 06708-645
www.macmillan.com.br
Atendimento ao professor: (11) 4613-2278
0800 16 88 77 (Outras regiões)
Fax: (11) 4612-6098

Impresso no Brasil - Gráfica Ave Maria - Janeiro/2015

1 Fill in the blanks with the correct forms of the verb *to be* in the present.

a Michael Phelps and Usain Bolt .... famous Olympic athletes. Phelps .... American and Bolt .... Jamaican.

b I .... good at all sports but I always participate in the competitions in my school.

c If you .... a soccer fan, why don't you try another sport such as volleyball or tennis?

d **A:** .... Diego Hypólito a Brazilian water polo athlete?

B: No, he .... He .... a Brazilian gymnast.

2 Choose the correct verb forms in parentheses to complete the text.

Olympic Villages

The 2016 Rio de Janeiro Olympic Games rely on two villages to host athletes and media professionals.

The Olympic and Paralympic Village (have / has) a scheduled completion date of 2015, a year before the games (takes / take) place. The original project (consists / consist) of 48 buildings 12 stories high with an overall accommodation capacity of 17,700 people. The future home of the athletes (is / are) near the Olympic Park, the main site of the competitions.

The project also (include / includes) the Athletes' Park, a leisure area for athletes. It is located in the recreational district, along with the Olympic and Paralympic Village. Incidentally, this is the first Rio-2016 facility to be completed. It was delivered in March 2012 and is already being used for sporting events by the population of Rio, even before becoming a legacy of the Games.

In addition to the Olympic and Paralympic Village, media professionals and referees who (attend / attends) the event also (have / has) their respective villages. Located in Rio's port area, the Media Village and the Referee Village (have / has) 1,800 apartments divided among 16 newly-erected buildings. After the Olympics, these units will be sold to Rio's civil servants.

Two other villages (are / is) to be completed for the Games and later will be sold to the citizens of Rio. The Green Village, in the district of Deodoro, (is / are) designed to house technical officials and support staff for sponsors. The Maracanã Village, in the district of the same name, (are / is) set aside for technical officials of the games.

Adapted from <http://www.brasil.gov.br>. Access on February 28, 2013.

3 Read the descriptions, find out, and write which Olympic sports they refer to.

    a A team sport that involves throwing a ball through a basket: ....

    b Two persons of similar weight competing to take control over each other: ....

    c An endurance event that consists of swimming, biking, and running: ....

    d Two or four players hit a lightweight ball back and forth, on a hard table, divided by a net: ....

    e Athletes attempt to lift a maximum weight: ....

Adapted from <www.databasesports.com>. Accessed on February 26, 2013.

4 Use the clues to make up questions in the present tense.

    a you / balanced / have / diet / a / ?

    ....

    b they / be / allergic to / any medication / ?

    ....

    c when / he / exercise / ?

    ....

    d I / be / apt / to play / table tennis / ?

    ....

    e she / need / to lose weight / ?

    ....

    f your metabolism / be / fast / ?

    ....

5 Now match the questions from exercise 4 to the answers below.

    ◯ Yes, and because of that I have a really hard time gaining weight.

    ◯ Sure! I only eat healthy food.

    ◯ Maybe she does! She's overweight.

    ◯ He swims three times a week, does that count?

    ◯ I'm sorry, but you can't play any sports before you take a medical evaluation.

    ◯ Yes, they are. They can't take penicillin.

6 **Write the descriptions in the box under the corresponding photos.**

> Alice is average height. Her hair is long, straight, and blonde.
>
> Amanda is short and chubby. She has long, wavy hair.
>
> Mr. Kent is dark-skinned, tall, and thin. He has short, curly hair.
>
> Miller is short and skinny.
>
> Sylvia is tall and fat.

a
....
....
....

b
....
....
....

c
....
....
....

e

....
....
....

f
....
....
....

I'm going through changes

1 Complete the table below with the comparative forms of the adjectives.

ambitious	
bad	
difficult	
dirty	
expensive	
fast	
good	
muscular	

2 Choose the right adjectives from the second column in exercise 1 to complete the dialogs below.

a **A:** Is math .... than history?

B: Sure! History is much easier.

b **A:** Which travels ....: a car or an airplane?

B: Of course cars are slower than airplanes!

c **A:** Amanda is .... than her sister Tereza.

B: Yes, she is. She never stops.

d **A:** Mark, go clean your room. It's .... than a pigsty!

B: All right, Mom. But it's not so bad… I even dusted the shelves this morning!

e **A:** What a marvelous car you have, Drake! I bet it's .... than my own house.

B: You're kidding, Ted! It's cheaper than you think.

f **A:** Boys who work out regularly are .... than those who exercise only on weekends.

B: You may be right, but being strong and athletic also depends on your body type.

3 Choose the correct options to fill in the blanks.

a School stress gets .... as teens move .... and have to accomplish more and more.

⭕ more great / more high   ⭕ greater / higher

b Parents often expect their teenage sons and daughters to be responsible for themselves and for their .... brothers and sisters as well.

⭕ more young   ⭕ younger

c Teens are generally .... about their performance in groups than adults.

⭕ more anxious   ⭕ anxious

d We often view teenagers as .... and immature when they're in groups.

⭕ criticaler   ⭕ more critical

e Parents should provide a .... and .... environment for their teens.

⭕ more healthy / more comprehensive   ⭕ healthier / more understanding

4 Read about these teenagers' problems. Use the comparative form of the adjectives in the box to complete the texts.

> healthy • intelligent • self-confident • shy • worried

a **A:** My brother thinks I'm........................... ....than he is because I like to study and read books but it's not true. He feels bad about it.

B: Explain to your brother that people are different and each person is better or worse at different skills. That doesn't mean some people are more intelligent than others, they are just different.

b **A:** I feel .... than usual when I'm next to a boy I like, and I don't know how to show what I'm feeling.

B: Talk to people who have the same problem, or ask your mom to teach you how to express your feelings in this situation. I'm sure you'll learn how to be .... next time!

c **A:** I get stomach cramps after eating junk food at school.

B: Always invest in .... foods.

d **A:** My dad doesn't allow me to go out with my friends at night.

B: Maybe it's because you're too young and he's .... about your safety than anything else.

5 Read Karine's blog. Then correct the statements, changing the adjectives. The first one is done for you.

Going Places

My kind of town

I prefer small towns to big cities for lots of reasons. First, because small towns are safer and friendlier; although life in big cities is more thrilling (I admit life in small towns may be boring sometimes), it is also more expensive and more stressful. As far as job opportunities are concerned, big cities offer better positions and higher salaries, but I opt to live a more modest but comfortable life in a small town. Big cities are noisier, more polluted, and also more violent than small towns, which provide us with closer contact with nature and, therefore, our well-being. And last but not least, people who live in small towns are more affectionate and lead a more peaceful life and that's what I want for my family.

Karine

Karine thinks that

a big cities are better than small towns.

big cities are worse than small towns.

b small towns are more dangerous than big cities.

....

c inhabitants of big cities lead a more peaceful life than those of small towns.

....

d life in small towns is more expensive than life in big cities.

....

e big cities are more boring than small towns.

....

f salaries in bigger cities are lower than in small towns.

....

Technology

1 **Check the correct verbs and complete the sentences.**

a Celena used to .... in love with every guy in our class.
○ fill   ○ fall

b In the past, that famous actor used to .... 5 to 8 movies a year.
○ shoot   ○ shut

c Uncle Tony used to .... me a bedtime story every night.
○ talk   ○ tell

d Grandma used to .... without her glasses before the surgery.
○ read   ○ repeat

e You used to .... jogging every day. Why don't you do that anymore?
○ get   ○ go

2 **Match the columns to form meaningful sentences.**

a Alice used to make her bed,

b Dad used to have a small car,

c I used to collect stamps,

d We didn't use to eat chocolate,

○ but I don't know where to find them anymore.

○ but now we are chocoholics.

○ but now he needs a bigger one to travel with the family.

○ but now she wakes up very early and her mother does that for her.

3 **Fill in the blanks with *used to* and the verbs in the box.**

> be • dream • lack • last • think • work

a Appliances .... energy-saving functions.

b In the past, major home appliances .... longer.

c Older motor and controller technology .... less efficiently than today's technology.

d In the 1950s, people .... that appliances like kettles and electric mixers were luxuries, but just a few years later, they were considered must-have items in everybody's kitchen.

e Washing machines .... bigger and heavier than they are nowadays.

4 Unscramble the words to form sentences.

a school / used to / of / some / in / make fun / high / others / students / .

....

b used to / time / my / same / younger / the / brother / at / TV / do / watch / his / and / homework / .

....

c talking / used to / I / in / nervous / feel / public / about / .

....

d used to / misbehave / children / at / Bart's / parties / .

....

e cable TV / video store / the / used to / movies / before / rent / at / lots of / we / .

....

f bigger / past / be / the / used to / cell phones / in / .

....

5 Use the information in parentheses to answer the questions.

a Who did you use to look up to 10 years ago? (my parents)

....

b Where did your relatives use to live? (in the suburbs)

....

c What did your brother use to play in kindergarten? (hide and seek)

....

d When did you and your boyfriend use to meet at the mall? (after school)

....

e How did Mary use to come to work? (by bus)

....

f How many books did you use to read a year? (five to eight)

....

6 Which electronics/technological devices are these? Write their names under the photos.

a

....

b

....

c

....

d

....

e

....

f

....

7 Choose the best option to describe the technology concepts below.

a A flash drive is
- ◯ a data storage device.
- ◯ a connection with no cables or wires.

b A broadband connection is
- ◯ a software operating system.
- ◯ a fast, permanent Internet connection.

c Text messages are
- ◯ short texts sent to and from cellular and smart phone devices.
- ◯ pictures, videos, or audios sent to and from computers.

d Wireless communication is
- ◯ a way to connect computer/communications equipment together without cables or wires.
- ◯ a way to connect computer/communications equipment together along with wires by means of electrical signals.

e A dead battery
- ◯ is no longer producing or functioning, it's discharged.
- ◯ crashes when your PC runs on a wireless connection.

Almanac mania

1 Fill in the blanks with *was* or *were* to complete the email Susan sent to her cousin Fred.

www.email_.com

To: Fred

From: Susan

Subject: My birthday

Hi, Fred!

It .... my birthday yesterday, and my family and I .... at our summer house with our friends. My parents planned a suprise in the afternoon, but it didn't really work out. They wanted to cut the cake and sing "Happy Birthday" at 3:00 pm, but my mom and sister .... still in the kitchen preparing our snacks. Dad .... near the pool keeping an eye on my younger brothers, and my friends .... in the game room. Where .... I? I .... at Grandma and Grandpa's side all the time as they .... afraid of my dogs! In the end, we had cake at 9:00 pm and went to bed!

Take care,

Susan

2 Choose the best alternatives to complete the dialogs.

a A: .... you at home yesterday afternoon?

B: No, we .... We .... in the library.

◯ Was / wasn't / were   ◯ Were / weren't / were

b A: What .... Kathy afraid of when she .... a child?

B: When she .... younger, she .... afraid of dogs. But not anymore!

◯ was / wasn't / was / wasn't   ◯ was / was / was / was

c A: Where .... you two after the game yesterday?

B: I .... in the restroom and Ted .... at the cafeteria. Why?

A: Because I .... lost and you .... there to help me!

◯ were / was / was / was / weren't   ◯ were / was / was / were / wasn't

3 Read the facts below. Then write the past forms of the verb *to be*.

a In 1885, Mark Twain's novel *The Adventures of Huckleberry Finn* .... published.

b Corinthians .... the World Soccer Champion in 2012.

c Rio de Janeiro .... the capital of Brazil from 1763 to 1960.

d John Travolta and Olivia Newton John .... the stars of the famous musical *Grease*.

e Brad Pitt and Friends actress Jennifer Aniston .... not married in 1998.

4 Read the definition of *almanac* provided by the *Encyclopedia Britannica* and a brief presentation of *The World Almanac of Books and Facts*. Then fill in the blanks with the words from the box.

> articles • astronomical • calendar • climate • countries
> election • facts • festivals • medieval • planets

Almanac

An almanac is a book or table containing a .... of the days, weeks, and months of the year; a record of various .... phenomena, often with .... information and seasonal suggestions for farmers; and miscellaneous other data. An almanac provides data on the rising and setting times of the Sun and Moon, the phases of the Moon, the positions of the ...., schedules of high and low tides, and a register of ecclesiastical .... and saints' days. The term *almanac* is of uncertain .... Arabic origin; in modern Arabic, *al-manākh* is the word for climate.

Extracted from <http://global.britannica.com>. Accessed on March 27, 2013.

The World Almanac and Book of Facts 2013 presents a reference with comprehensive .... and statistics on current events, people and the .... of the world, along with 2012 U.S. presidential .... results, and original .... on recent issues and topics.

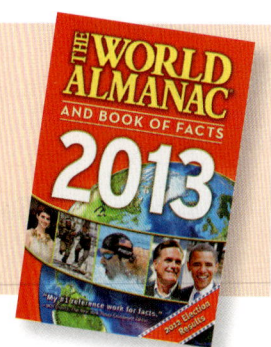

Reproduced from <www.npr.org>. Accessed on March 28, 2013.

5 Rewrite the sentences below using the verb *to be* in the past. Replace the information in italics with the words / expressions in parentheses.

a Carla and Erica are sick *today*. (yesterday)

....

b I'm not tired *now*. (in the morning)

....

c Are you on the phone *at the moment*? (earlier)

....

d Why is Amy so quiet *right now*? (last night)

....

e We are neighbors *today*. (in 2010)

....

6 Use the cues to write questions and answers using the Simple Past of the verb *to be*. The first one is done for you.

a Almanacs / popular / in 2001 / in the 70s

A: Were almanacs popular in 2001?

B: No, they weren't. They were popular in the 70s.

b *The World Almanac* / first published in Greece / in the U.S.A.

A: ....

B: ....

c fashion and media data / in the first almanac issues / agricultural, astronomical, and meteorological data

A: ....

B: ....

d Deborah / interested in sports almanacs / interested in economics and business almanacs

A: ....

B: ....

e Almanaque Sadol / distributed in Colombia / distributed in Brazil

A: ....

B: ....

Everyday mythology

1 Complete the sentences. Choose the correct adjectives from the box.

> ambitious • curious • friendly • romantic • strong

a Hera was a .... goddess. She was always helping people.

b Midas was an .... king. He loved gold.

c Achilles was a .... warrior. His ankles were the vulnerable part of his body.

d Cupid was so ....! He's still the symbol of love nowadays.

e Pandora was such a .... person. She opened the mysterious box.

2 Now match the sentences from exercise 1 to the real life situations in the photos below.

3 Choose the correct endings for these sentences about Greek mythology.

a Everything King Midas touched
○ was transformed into gold.   ○ was transformed into garbage.

b Narcissus was
○ an ugly man who was in love with a goddess.
○ a handsome man who was in love with himself.

c The Trojan Horse was
○ King Leonidas's favorite horse.   ○ a big wooden horse with soldiers inside.

d Achilles' mother dipped
○ him into a magical river.   ○ him into a dirty river.

e Morpheus was
○ the god of sleep and dreams.   ○ the god of music and dance.

f Pan was
○ the god of foods and gestures.   ○ the god of woods and pastures.

4 Write the sentences in the past using *was, wasn't, were* or *weren't.*

    a There .... a wooden horse in the Trojan War. (affirmative)

    b There .... a king called Ambrosius. (negative)

    c There .... gods and demigods in Greek mythology. (affirmative)

    d There .... strong female goddesses. (negative)

5 Complete the questions with the right form of *there to be.* Then answer them.

    a .... stories about mythological monsters?

    Yes, ...

    b .... a friendly god?

    Yes, ...

    c .... gods inside the Trojan Horse?

    No, ...

    d .... a goddess named Pandora?

    No, ...

6 Complete the sentences with *there was / there wasn't, there were / there weren't.* Then, match both columns.

    a .... a statue of Zeus on Mount Olympus.

    b .... real gods.

    c .... many demigods.

    d .... a warrior like Achilles.

    ◯ They're all myths.

    ◯ He was the king of the gods.

    ◯ He was very brave and intelligent.

    ◯ Some gods had kids with mortals.

7 List three things that have changed in your city in the last five years. Use the right form of *there to be* to write about your memories. There is an example for you.

There was a photo shop in front of the bakery.

....

....

....

....

....

....

....

....

8 Jennie is telling Tom about a furniture store she has been to. Complete the dialog between them with there to be in the past.

Tom: Hi, Jennie! How was the furniture store?

Jennie: Oh, I loved it! Especially one showroom. .... beautiful furniture in this living room.

Tom: .... an armchair?

Jennie: Yes, ... A blue one. .... a lovely red sofa, too, and .... two gray pillows on it.

Tom: .... any tables?

Jennie: Yes, ... two: a central table and a small one beside the armchair, with a lamp on it.

Tom: .... pictures on the wall?

Jennie: No, ... But there was a white bookshelf with different objects on it. Cool! And .... a lovely beige rug on the floor.

The young and talented

1 Write the superlatives of the adjectives below.

expensive	
fat	
good	
happy	
important	
intelligent	
smart	
tall	
tired	
young	

2 Circle the odd one out.

a fastest – smartest – most intelligent – fast

b young – modern – well – fine

c worried – healthiest – oldest – most successful

d quiet – silly – ugly – softly

3 Complete the sentences with the superlative form of the adjectives in parentheses.

a She is the .... student in school. (tall)

b They are always the .... players of the team. (tired)

c Paulo is the .... piano player in the world. (young)

d Silvio was the .... runner in the competition. (slow)

e Patrick is the .... cook in his family. (good)

f Carmen is the .... girl at the party. (happy)

4 Write sentences with the words given. Use superlatives. The first one is done for you.

a Paul / good / doctor / in town

Paulo is the best doctor in town.

b Chocolate ice cream / delicious / dessert / in my opinion

....

c The Beatles / famous / band / in the 60's

....

d Marcos / healthy / person / I know

....

e Susan / pretty / woman / in the neighborhood

....

f The Meridien / expensive / hotel / in Vancouver

....

5 Read the clues and complete the sentences with the professions in the box.

cook • doorkeeper • engineer • hairdresser • police officer • waiter

a My mother has a very dangerous profession. She investigates crimes and protects people in town. She's a ....

b My aunt cuts, colors, and arranges the hair of lots of women every day. She's a ....

c My boyfriend loves his job. He works at a restaurant, serving food and drinks. He's a ....

d My grandfather built that church. He was an ....

e My father is an excellent .... Everybody loves the delicious pasta he makes.

f The .... who works in my building is so friendly! He always opens the door with a big smile.

6 Choose the correct form of the superlative of the adjectives to complete the sentences.

a Usain Bolt is the .... man on Earth.
- ◯ fastest
- ◯ most fast

b Albert Einstein was the .... scientist of the twentieth century.
- ◯ famousest
- ◯ most famous

c Mozart was the .... young composer of his time. He was a child prodigy.
- ◯ most talented
- ◯ talentedest

7 Read the headlines and choose the correct alternatives to complete them.

a

The _____ Jobs in America
- By STEVEN GREENHOUSE -

12:27 p.m. | Updated

- ◯ most dangerous
- ◯ dangerest
- ◯ more dangerest

b

UK moves into _____ nations top ten

Robert Lea   Last updated at 9:18AM, May 28 2013

- ◯ most happier
- ◯ happiest
- ◯ more happier

c

PRODIGY, 21, BECOMES _____ MD* FROM UNIV. OF CHICAGO

Associated Press
Updated 6/5/2012 10:42:48 AM ET

- ◯ most younger
- ◯ youngest
- ◯ more youngest

*MD = Medical Doctor

1 **What are they wearing? Match the pictures to the descriptions.**

a

○ He's wearing a white shirt with a tie.

b

○ He's wearing a checked jacket.

○ She's wearing sunglasses.

c

d

○ She's wearing a light color dress.

e

○ He's wearing baggy Bermudas, T-shirt, and a cap.

f

○ She's wearing a skirt, a blouse, and sandals.

2 **What do you wear most? Write about your favorite clothes.**

....

....

3 **Complete the questions with *who, when* or *where*.**

a .... did the Black Power movement happen?
It happened between the 1950s and 1960s.

b .... did the Black Power movement start?
It started in the United States.

c .... was the first Brazilian celebrity to assume the Black Power style?
It was Toni Tornado.

4 Read the texts about these two American artists and fill in the blanks with *who* or *which*.

MICHAEL JACKSON

"The King of Pop" is the nickname he was given, ... was a well-deserved one. Michael Jackson was a performing singer .... had many styles. One of his most remarkable performances was his "moonwalk" steps, ... he executed with stunning perfection at the Motown 25th Anniversary special. .... would say that little kid from "Jackson Five" would grow up to be such an amazing artist?

STEVIE WONDER

Stevie Wonder, ... was born on May 13, 1950, is an American singer, songwriter, and multi-instrumentalist. He visited Brazil many times, and performed with Gilberto Gil in a free Christmas concert .... took place at Rio's Copacabana beach in 2012.

5 Make sentences with the information given. Use *who* or *which*. The first one is done for you.

a Social medias / a kind of networking service / used to connect people
Social medias are a kind of networking service which are used to connect people.

b Justin Bieber / singer / perform all over the world

....

c New York / tourist destination / perfect for shopping

....

d The cheetah / feline / the fastest animal in the world

....

e Ashton Kutcher / actor / famous for movies and TV series

....

f William Bonner and Fatima Bernardes / Brazilian journalists / have triplets.

....

6 Read the text about President Barack Obama's life and answer the questions. Give full answers.

President Barack Obama
Barack H. Obama is the 44th President of the United States.

His story is the American story – values from the heartland, a middle-class upbringing in a strong family, hard work and education as the means of getting ahead, and the conviction that a life so blessed should be lived in service to others.

With a father from Kenya and a mother from Kansas, President Obama was born in Hawaii on August 4, 1961. He was raised with help from his grandfather, who served in Patton's army, and his grandmother, who worked her way up from the secretarial pool to middle management at a bank.

He went on to attend law school, where he became the first African-American president of the *Harvard Law Review*. Upon graduation, he returned to Chicago to help lead a voter registration drive, teach constitutional law at the University of Chicago, and remain active in his community.

Extracted from <www.whitehouse.gov>. Accessed on April 5, 2013.

a Was Barack Obama's father American?

....

b Who helped raise him?

....

c What did he achieve at law school?

....

d What did he do at the University of Chicago?

....

7 Choose a famous African-American or Afro-Brazilian you admire. Then write a paragraph with information about him/her (name, nationality, famous for).

....

....

....

....

....

....

Homemade gifts

1 **Complete the sentences with *some* or *any*.**

a Aunt Georgia gives us .... homemade gifts every Christmas.

b There aren't .... stickers left.

c Is there .... glue to make the card?

d You need .... paper to do this activity.

e There aren't .... presents under the Christmas tree.

f Are there .... birthday cards in that drawer?

2 **Look at he photos and complete the sentences with the correct words. Use *some* and *any* accordingly.**

cupcakes   scrapbooks   origami   piñatas

a At my cousin's birthday party in Mexico, there weren't .... She doesn't like them.

b .... shapes are really difficult to fold. For me, it's pretty hard to make shapes out of paper.

c What a delicious smell! I bet Grandma has .... ready for us.

d I don't have .... I want to make my own with memories of important moments in my life.

3 **Unscramble the words to form sentences. Use *some* and *any*.**

a good ideas / on the Internet / there are / of homemade gifts / .

....

b don't / to make / you / a Christmas card /need / help / .

....

c suggestions / in the box / are there / ?

....

d people / to make/ prefer / their own Christmas presents / .

....

4 **Choose the best alternative and complete the sentence.**

a In Brazil, we usually buy .... for family and friends at Christmastime.

○ gifts

○ piñatas

b In the United States, people usually .... for Valentine's Day.

○ fold origami

○ make cards

c .... is an alternative in order to spend less money on presents.

○ big Christmas parties

○ Secret Santa

d A personalized .... is an excellent homemade gift for friends who love reading.

○ bookmark

○ scrapbook

5 **Complete the handcraft crossword. Use the clues to help you.**

DOWN

1 Colored paper used to wrap presents.

2 Great for painting gifts.

3 Thick paper used to make cards.

ACROSS

4 Perfect to cut lots of paper at the same time.

5 Used to stick things together.

6 Classify the words into countable or uncountable. Write them in the correct place.

> glitter • glue • marker • paint
> paper • photo • ribbon • sticker

Countable: ....

Uncountable: ....

7 Match the cards and the messages.

a
Happy Birthday!

◯ May you have many years of love and happiness together!

b
Happy Valentine's day!

◯ It's time to celebrate your new age! I wish you plenty of wonderful moments!

c
Merry Christmas!

◯ Light the candles and decorate the tree. May the season bring you gifts of love and joy.

d
Happy Wedding Wishes!

◯ You're always in my heart! Your friendship is a valuable treasure.

8 Answer the questions about gift traditions. Give full answers.

a Which gift traditions does your family keep?

....

b Does anyone in your family usually make gifts instead of buying them?

....

c About the different traditions on page 123 of your book, which one(s) do you like most?

....

d Which of these different gift traditions do you think is the most fun?

....

http://kidshealth.org

For Teens

Why Are Self-Esteem and Body Image Important?

Self-esteem is all about how much you feel you are worth — and how much you feel other people value you. Self-esteem is important because feeling good can affect your mental health and how you behave.

People with high self-esteem know themselves well. They're realistic and find friends that like and appreciate them for who they are. People with high self-esteem usually feel more in control of their lives and know their own **strengths** and **weaknesses**.

Body image is how you see your physical self — including if you feel you are attractive and if others like your **looks**. For many people, especially people in their early teens, body image is associated with self-esteem.

What Influences a Person's Self-Esteem?

Adolescence and Development

Some people battle with their self-esteem and body image when they begin puberty (or adolescence) because it's a time when the body goes through many changes. These changes, and the wish to feel accepted by our friends, means it can be a temptation to compare ourselves with others. The problem with that is, not everyone grows or develops at the same time or in the same way.

Media Images and Other Outside Influences

Our tweens (between the ages 8 to 12) and early teens (between the ages of 12 and 15) are a time when we become more familiar with **celebrities** and media images — as well as how other kids look and how adequate or adapted we are. We might start to make comparisons with other people or media images ("ideals" that are frequently made prettier than they really are). All of this can affect how we feel even as we grow into our teens.

Families and School

Family life can sometimes influence our body image. Some parents or **coaches** can be too focused on looking a certain way or meeting some needed weight for a sports team. Family members sometimes progress with difficulty with their own body image or criticize their kids' looks ("why do you wear your hair so long?" or "how come you can't wear pants that are your size?"). This can all influence a people's self-esteem, especially if they're sensitive to other peoples' comments or affected by other people's opinions.

Adapted from http://kidshealth.org. Accessed on April 10, 2013.

1 **Check the correct alternatives according to the text.**

a ◯ If you have a positive body image, you don't accept yourself the way you are and want to be like some media ideal at all costs.

b ◯ Making good friends and becoming more independent from one's parents are aspects a person with low self-esteem shows.

c ◯ The need to feel accepted by friends drives teenagers to compare themselves with others.

d ◯ Family criticism about looks can influence a person's self-esteem.

e ◯ Possessing low self-esteem can make people more in control of their lives.

f ◯ Body image refers to a person's feelings about the attractiveness of his or her body.

2 **Complete the sentences with the words from the box, according to the text.**

> body image • ideals • opinions • puberty • self-esteem • teenagers

a .... is a time when the body goes through many changes.

b Media images or .... set standards that are not real, but the media makes it seems easy for us to live up to these ideals.

c Your .... reflects how you feel about the way you look.

d Your behavior and your mental health are affected by your ....

e Especially for ...., body image and self-esteem are very connected.

f When a person is easily affected by other people's ...., his / her body image can also be affected easily.

3 **Find the words in bold in the text that correspond to the following definitions.**

a ....: intellectual or moral forces; power of resistance, as in a person's character.

b ....: physical appearance, especially when pleasing.

c ....: famous people.

d ....: people who train or direct athletes or athletic teams.

e ....: deficiencies or failings, as in a person's character.

Definitions adapted from www.thefreedictionary.com. Accessed on April 10, 2013.

Extra Reading 2

Status

Why Facebook Makes You Feel Bad about Yourself

No surprise — those Facebook photos of your friends on vacation or celebrating a birthday party can make you feel horrible.

Facebook is supposed to be used to connect with friends and maybe find people who are interesting to you, and looking over friends' pages is supposed to make us feel loved, supported and important (at least in the lives of those we like). But examining photos of friends' life successes can cause feelings of envy, misery and loneliness as well, according to researchers from two German universities. The scientists studied 600 people who spent time on the social network and discovered that one in three felt worse after visiting the site — especially if they viewed vacation photos. Facebook frequenters who spent time on the site without posting their own content were also more probable to feel dissatisfied.

"We were surprised by how many people have a negative experience from Facebook as the feeling of resentment (or envy) because you don't have something your friend has makes them feel lonely, frustrated or angry," study author Hanna Krasnova from the Institute of Information Systems at Berlin's Humboldt University told Reuters. "From our observations some of these people then leave Facebook or at least reduce their use of the site."

The most common cause of Facebook frustration comes from users comparing themselves socially to their fellows, while the second most common origin of dissatisfaction was "lack of attention" from having fewer comments, likes and general feedback than their friends.

The study authors note that both men and women feel pressure to describe their moments as the best ones ever to their Facebook friends, but men are more inclined to post more self-promotional content in their "About Me" and "Notes" sections than women, who tend to stress their physical glamor and friendliness.

In general shared content does not have to be "explicitly bragging or exultant" for envy feelings to come out. In fact, a lonely user can feel resentment or pain because of the numerous birthday wishes his more sociable friend receives on his FB Wall. In the same way, a friend's change in the relationship status from "single" to "in a relationship" can cause emotional chaos for someone who is not in a relationship.

So far, there are more positive effects of being socially connected than negative consequences of feeling inferior or left out by your circle of friends. But the authors suggest that if the suffering feelings grow, Facebook and other social media can no longer be a fun way to stay connected with friends, but can become just another origin of stress for people.

Adapted from http://healthland.time.com. Accessed on April 10, 2013.

1 **Match the columns according to the text.**

a According to studies,

b The good aspects of social connections are more numerous than

c People who have a negative experience from Facebook

d Absence of attention

e Someone who is going through relationship problems

f After all, social medias

◯ the negative effects such as feeling inferior, for example.

◯ either leave the network or reduce their use of the site.

◯ can feel envy if he or she sees a friend's change of status from "single" to "in a relationship".

◯ one in three people who visited Facebook felt worse after they viewed vacation photos.

◯ can become one extra problem for users.

◯ is the second most common reason for dissatisfaction with Facebook.

2 **Write true (T) or false (F).**

a Facebook's objective is to make us feel miserable, unimportant, and unloved. ◯

b Simple birthday wishes may become a reason for people's envy to come out. ◯

c Looking over friends' pages always makes us feel loved. ◯

d When pain and suffering come from the use of Facebook, all users tend to connect to other social networks immediately. ◯

e Facebook users who spent a long time posting their successes were unhappy. ◯

f Having fewer likes than your friends can be a reason for Facebook frustration. ◯

3 **Below are general comments about Facebook. Are they positive (P) or negative (N) aspects?**

a There's no real interaction among those who we call friends and we can have a false idea of what friendship really is. ◯

b It is a way to keep in touch with our family and friends who live far away. ◯

c When users are in a relationship, Facebook can arouse jealousy and tension between partners and even cause breakups. ◯

d Because users compare themselves to others, Facebook causes insecurities. ◯

e A lot of people think it's easier to start a conversation with someone in Facebook than in real life, so a lot of friendships can start there. ◯

f If users do not set their profiles to private, anyone can have access to every piece of information they decide to share. ◯

Extra Reading 3

GREEK MYTHOLOGY IN CONTEXT

UXL Encyclopedia of World Mythology, 2009

The mythology of the ancient Greeks includes a great collection of gods, demigods (half-human, half-god), monsters, and heroes. Greek mythology became part of European culture, and many of its stories became known around the world.

Greek gods and goddesses were much like people, but with wonderful powers. Their actions resulted from passions, such as pride, jealousy, love, and the thirst for revenge. The deities (gods) used to leave Mount Olympus to become involved in the affairs of mortals, interacting with men and women as protectors, enemies, and sometimes lovers. They were not above using tricks and disguises to influence events, and their schemes and plots often involved people.

Heroes and ordinary humans in Greek myths frequently discovered that things were not what they appeared to be. The basic moral principle was that the gods rewarded honorable behavior and obedience, and people who dishonored themselves or defied the gods usually paid a high price.

Greek mythology is a combination of stories, some conflicting with one another. The ancient beliefs joined up with legends from Greek kingdoms and city-states and myths borrowed from other peoples to form a body of lore shared by most Greeks.

For hundreds of years, these myths passed from generation to generation in spoken form. Then, around the time of the classical Greek culture of the city-states, people began writing them down. The works of Hesiod and Homer are key origins for the mythology of ancient Greece. Hesiod's *Theogony* tells of creation and of the gods' origins and relationships. The epic poems *Iliad* and *Odyssey* show the gods influencing human fortunes. In addition, Pindar wrote poems called odes that contain much myth and legend.

Non-Greek sources also exist. The Romans dominated the Mediterranean world after the Greeks and adopted elements of Greek mythology. The Roman poet Ovid's poem *Metamorphoses* retells many Greek myths.

Adapted from http://ic.galegroup.com. Accessed on April 10, 2013.

1 **Which statement is NOT false?**

a Demigods were never part of the mythology of the ancient Greeks. ◯

b Greek myths never conflict one another. ◯

c European culture doesn't accept Greek mythology. ◯

d Gods were very different from people in general. ◯

e Greek gods sometimes used tricks to get what they wanted. ◯

2 **Choose the correct alternatives to complete the sentences about the text.**

a We can find more than one version of a myth in Greek mythology

◯ because it's a mixture of stories and myths from other peoples.

◯ because the gods interacted with mortals.

b Myths represent human belief, fantasy, and creativity,

◯ but they're not part of our cultural world nowadays.

◯ and that's why they're still popular nowadays.

c Ancient beliefs, legends, and myths

◯ defy the gods and pay a high price for that.

◯ form a collective knowledge or wisdom on mythology.

d Greek gods were very much like humans

◯ and were vulnerable to human emotions.

◯ but never involved people in their plots.

e The fundamental moral principles of Greek myths are

◯ honorable behavior and obedience.

◯ monsters and heroes.

3 **Read the definitions and choose the correct idiom.**

a *It's all Greek to me / All roads lead to Rome*: this idiom refers to something that is incomprehensible or undecipherable.

b *Rome wasn't built in a day / When in Rome, do as the Romans do*: this proverb refers to the way a person should behave, that is, like those around him or her.

c *It's all Greek to me / Rome wasn't built in a day*: it takes time to do great things.

d *All roads lead to Rome / When in Rome, do as the Romans do*: it means that there are many ways to reach the same goal.

Adapted from http://www.ancientl.com. Accessed on April 10, 2013.